YOUR KNOWLEDGE HAS VALUE

- We will publish your bachelor's and master's thesis, essays and papers

- Your own eBook and book - sold worldwide in all relevant shops

- Earn money with each sale

Upload your text at www.GRIN.com
and publish for free

Sven Elmers

A critical analysis of Google's behavior towards its users in relation to the EU Data Protection Act and the US Safe Harbour Act

GRIN Publishing

Imprint:

Copyright © 2009 GRIN Verlag GmbH
Print and binding: Books on Demand GmbH, Norderstedt Germany
ISBN: 978-3-656-04233-4

This book at GRIN:

http://www.grin.com/en/e-book/181275/a-critical-analysis-of-google-s-behavior-
towards-its-users-in-relation

GRIN - Your knowledge has value

Since its foundation in 1998, GRIN has specialized in publishing academic texts by students, college teachers and other academics as e-book and printed book. The website www.grin.com is an ideal platform for presenting term papers, final papers, scientific essays, dissertations and specialist books.

Visit us on the internet:

http://www.grin.com/

http://www.facebook.com/grincom

http://www.twitter.com/grin_com

New College Durham

"A CRITICAL ANALYSIS OF GOOGLE'S BEHAVIOUR TOWARDS ITS USERS IN RELATION TO THE EUROPEAN DATA PROTECTION ACT AND THE UNITED STATES SAFE HARBOR ACT"

By
Sven Elmers

Dissertation submitted in fulfilment of the project unit for the degree of:

BA (HONS) MANAGEMENT, BUSINESS AND ADMINISTRATION

Submission Date: 18/05/2009

Glossary of terms

IP   - Internet protocol

An identifier for a computer or device on a network. The format of an IP address is a 32-bit numeric address written as four numbers separated by periods.

URL   - Universal resource locator

Global address of documents and other resources on the world wide web.

EFF   - Electronic Frontier Foundation

A foundation dealing with internet, computer and privacy issues.

VOIP - Voice over internet protocol

VOIP refers to the use of IP to transfer voice communications in much the same way that web pages and e-mails are transferred. Each piece of voice data is digitized in to chunks and then sent across the internet. With VOIP people can make calls over the internet as well as to regular phones and mobile phones.

ECHR- European Convention on Human Rights

EULA - End user license agreement

Type of license used for most software. An EULA is a legal contract between the manufacturer and/or the author and the end user of an application.

EPIC - Electronic Privacy Information Center

EPIC is a public interest research center in Washington, D.C. It was established in 1994 to focus public attention on emerging civil liberties issues and to protect privacy.

GPS - Global positioning system

GPS is a worldwide satellite navigational system.

4

The abstract

The researcher chose the title "A critical analysis of Google's behaviour towards its users in relation to the European Data Protection Act and the United States Safe Harbor Act" because Google is under the criticism of experts, institutions as well as governments of infringing several data protection acts.
The purpose of the project is to analyse to what extent Google is infringing the European Data Protection Act of 12 July, 2002 and/or the United States Safe Harbor Act of July, 2000 (as well as any other EU and US laws that apply) and to analyse to what extent Google users are aware of the criticisms surrounding Google.

Background information for the reader, especially in terms of privacy and the criticism that exists about Google can be found in the literature review. The methodolgy explains the research techniques that the author used for his project.

The main findings from the research are the following:
Although Google is hardly criticised and the author's primary research findings prove the criticism that exists about Google is not without cause, the secondary research findings about the laws of the Data Protection Acts of the European Union and of the United States of America, prove that Google is adhering to these Acts and that the criticism surrounding Google privacy law issues are not valid. Furthermore, the primary research findings show that the criticism about Google in most cases either does not have an impact on the loyalty of their customers because of a strong brand name and the focusing on the user experience or because users are not aware of the criticism surrounding Google.

Table of contents

Chapter 1
Introduction

1.1 The rationale for this research

Over the past years, the internet grew rapidly and became a very important in-
dustry. In order to save time and cost, people use search engines such as
Google, MSN or Lycos.

According to Kaumanns, R. (2007), the largest of all search engines is the
Google Search Engine. Google offers besides its search engine also applications
such as Street View, Maps, Docs, Calendar and more which are all free to use.
However, lots of criticism is published about Google on the internet and in a privacy ranking of internet service companies of Privacy International in 2007
(privacyinternational.org, 2007), Google ranked last in terms of privacy for customers. Therefore, the researcher elected the title "A critical analysis of Google's
behaviour in relation to the European Data Protection Act and the United States
Safe Harbor Act"

The author wants to research, if and to what extent Google is infringing the laws,
especially the European Data Protection Act of 12 July, 2002 and/or the United
States Safe Harbor Act of July, 2000 by including user-sensitive data in their
search results and by saving and sending all user enquiries and data to Google,
as well as to research some cases in particular, such as Google Street View in
relation to the European Charter of Fundamental Rights of December, 2000.
Furthermore, he wants to analyse Google's customer awareness and behaviour
and to find out why Google is, despite criticism, so popular.

1.2 The objectives of this research

In order to meet the aim of this research, the author set the following objectives:

1. Identification of reasons why Google is, despite criticism, so popular.

With this objective, the researcher wants to assess to what extent Google users are aware of the criticism surrounding Google.
Why are millions of people using Google, although the company is hardly critici-sed for their lack of data protection for individuals?

2. Evaluation on the relationship between how Google works with user-sensitive data and in what way the company depends on these data for their business.

These are two seperate issues that are combined with each other to demonstrate Google's need to collect data.
Is Google legally allowed to work and earn money with data of others?

3. Critical analysis of Google's behaviour in relation to the European Data Protec-tion Act and the United States Safe Harbor Act (among other laws)

The author wants to compare the criticism with the legal situation (Eurpean Data Protection Act of 12 July, 2002 and the United States Safe Harbor Act of July 2000, as well as Human Rights Acts) and to demonstrate by executing an expe-riment if an individual has the ability to find sensitive information about a certain person, and if so, how much can be found?

4. Analysis of Google's customer awareness and behaviour.

The author aims to discuss Google's customer awareness and behaviour with the participants of the experiment and to analyse and evaluate the customer be-

haviour - this is in relation to the first and third objective. He wants to find out how the customers of Google feel about the stealing of data and data protection in particular.

5. Recommendations for Google's customers to protect their data.

This objective is in relation to the outcomes of the experiment mentioned in the third objective. If our society is very transparent when it comes to the internet, how can I improve my safety on the internet and protect my data?

1.3 Chapter overview

First, the author presents the literature review with a conclusion about the criticism about Google to give background information to the reader. Theory, such as privacy in general and the legislation will also be part of the literature review. Second, the author presents the methodology with the research strategies, approaches, techniques, families and the general key concept of research. The intention is to explain and justify how the Project will be carried out.

Then follows the main body with the analysis of primary and secondary research findings, such the comparison of Google's behaviour to the European Data Protection Act and to the United States Safe Harbor Act, the evaluation on how Google works with user data and the outcomes of the questionnaire and experiment as well as the evaluation of Google's customer behaviour. This section will be divided by objectives.

The last chapter is the conclusion with a review of research objectives, followed by the appendices.

Chapter 2
Literature Review

2.1 The Internet

Internet technologies are changing our everyday lives. Through the history it constantly brought new innovations and made our lives easier in terms of access, time management and control. Billions of websites are available for access. According to comScore.com, 29.7 billion webpages were counted, with a growth rate of 6 million webpages per day in 2007. (comScore.com, 2007)

"The internet offers a lot of crap, but the rest is pretty good actually"
(Zittrain, J., 2008, p.9)

In order to optimize information, user can use online search engines. According to a com Score survey, Google is the most popular and leading search engine among internet user. (comScore.com, 2007)

This literature review presents a conclusion of articles and sections of books on the criticism about Google. These statements reflect the main issues about Google in the news which made the author do this project and are needed in order to understand the purpose of this project. Moreover, the researcher will give theoretical principles such as the Data Protection Legislation and privacy in general.

2.2 Data protection: Google is comming under criticism

"The Google-Economy: How Google changes the economy" by Kaumanns, R. (2007) explains how Google is in the focus of data protection specialists. The company has been ranked in an investigation of Privacy International among 23 internet companies on last place (privacyinternational.org, 2007). According to the investigation, Google has a profound aversion against privacy. Furthermore,

Google collects a vast quantity of data from their user to make it internationally accessible to the whole world. Privacy International is accusing Google of the growing possibilities to invade in the private sphere of user, as well as the lack of empowerment for user to control or delete their data.

"We raised concerns regarding the dangers and privacy implications of having a centrally-located, widely popular data warehouse of millions of Internet users' searches, and how under controversial existing U.S. law, Google can be forced to hand over all such information to the U.S. government."

(EFF, Criticism about Google, 2007)

"Our mission is to organize the world's information and make it universally accessible and useful"

(google.com/corporate, 2009)

In terms of time management and access, Google helps millions of people around the world everyday but according to Kaumanns, search enquiries will be saved and sent to Google in conclusion with other user data. (Kaumanns, R., 2007) Kaumanns also says that their EULAs are infringing several Data Protection Acts, because in paragraph 11 they are stating that the user give Google a perpetual, irrevocable, worldwide, royalty-free and non-exclusive licence to reproduce, adapt, modify, translate, publish, publicly perform, publicly display and distribute any content that the user submit, post or display on or through Google's services. This licence agreement applies for Google's browser Chrome.

"Google's new web browser Chrome is fast, shiny, and requires users to sign their very lives over to Google before they can use it. Today's Internet outrage du jour has been Chrome's EULA, which appears to give Google a nonexclusive right to display and distribute every bit of content transmitted through the browser."

(Arstechnica.com, From the News Desk, 2008)

"Germans Towns saying "Nein" to Google Street View"
(San Francisco Chronicle, October issue, 2008)

Half naked people, nose picker, people in front of a porn movie theater, all clue-
less photographed and included in Google Street View. According to the German
Representative for Data Protection, Peter Schaar, the collected photographs and
the implementation in Google Street View are infringing the German data protection act. According to him, viewers can get an optical imagination about nature,
buildings, the outer shape of houses and backyards and can imagine about furni-
ture, value, accessibility and the possibility for theft. (bfdi.bund.de, 2008)

In Germany, as well as in lots of other European countries, Google stopped the
aquisition of residences of properties because of governmental restrictions for
now. (google.com/privacy, 2009)

According to the EFF, data protection moved from a secondary concern to a con-
tentious political system.

John Perry Barlow, a member of the EFF is said that *"Relying on the government
to protect our privacy is like asking a peeping tom to install your window blinds."*

He argues that governments can only set general restrictions, such as the shut down of Google Street View in Europe, or introduce new ammendments to the law but they cannot give restrictions for each website and. He says that people have to care themselves about their data and their privacy by trying to control it.

According to Blakley, B. (1999), the flow of data is immense and cannot be controlled by people. He says that new software is needed in order to protect systems and sensitive data.

2.3 Privacy

"European regulators found that companies such as Google and Yahoo violate data protection acts by ..." (Ryan Singel, Member of the EFF, eff.org, 2008) Privacy is a fundamental human right. The United Nations Declaration of Human Rights defined privacy as the following:

"No one shall be subjected to arbitrary interference with his privacy, family, home or correspondence, nor to attacks upon his honour and reputation. Everyone has the right to the protection of the law against such interference or attacks."

Bob Blakley, a principal analyst of the Burton Group stated that *"Privacy is not the right to be left alone - I don't want to be alone, but I still want privacy. Furthermore, privacy is not anonymity - If I'm anonymous, I don't need privacy."* (Blakley, B., 1999, p. 53)

Article 8 of the European Convention of Human Rights states that *"Everyone has the right to respect for his private and family life, his home and his correspondence. There shall be no interference by a public authority with the exercise of this right except such as is in accordance with the law and is necessary in a democratic society in the interests of national security, public safety or the economic well-being of the country, for the prevention of disorder or crime, for the protection of health or morals, or for the protection of the rights and freedoms of others."*

According to Zittrain, on one hand, Human Right Acts and Data Protection Legislation regulate Privacy, on the other hand freedom without privacy does not exist,
because if everything one says and thinks is exposed one does not really have
freedom. According to him, technology gave the tools and security concerns gave
the legitimacy to keep track of everything one does. (Zittrain, J., 2008)

Google's mission statement is *"to organize the world's information and make it
universally accessible and useful."* (google.com/corporate, 2009)

According to Ray Everett-Church (2008, p. 201), an expert on privacy laws, this
statement has no qualifiers, because *"Google is not limiting itself to the information that only people want organized and accessible, nor do they suggest limiting
accessibility to anything that somebody should not accessing."*

Chapter 3
Methodology

3.1 Key Concepts of Research

"Methodology is the theory of how research should be undertaken, including the theoretical and philosophical assumption upon which research is based and the implication of these for the method or methods adopted"

(Saunders, M., 2000, p. 62)

In order to investigate the research question and to archieve the objectives mentioned in the purpose of the research, the author needed to make a choice of how to implement the reseach families, methods and different approaches appropriately as well as to be sure of the reliability and validity of the results.

Before research, the author set clear objectives and defined the most effective and relevant methodology, which helped the author in order to get an accurate and informative project outcome. Furthermore, it helped him to explain the research question in regard to the objectives in more detail. Because this research involved a lot of content and different opinions and views, it was important to put emphasis on triangulation, because of possible threats to validity.

3.1.1. Validity

"Validity has to do with whether your methods, approaches and techniques actually relate to, or measure, the issue you have been exploring"

(Blaxter, L., 2006, p. 44)

Emphasis had to be put on validity, because the validity is about correctness and therefore the author had to put also a lot of emphasis on reliable sources. The validity of data can be improved by using triangulation.

3.1.2 Triangulation

"...the term triangulation refers to obtaining evidence from multiple sources to ensure that a biased view is not being obtained from one informant."

(Remenyi, D., 1998, p. 145)

Triangulation involves the practice of viewing things from more than one perspective. This can mean the use of different methods, different sources of data or even different researchers within the study. (Denscombe, M., 2007, p.134)
All information should be linked to each other in order to get the best outcome. To check the validity of information, the author made use of more that one research technique and collected different types of data from reliable sources.

3.1.3 Reliability

"A good level of reliability means that the research instrument produces the same data time after time on each occasion that it is used, and that any variation in the results obtained through using the instrument is due entirely to variations in the thing being measured. None of the variation is due to fluctuations caused by the volatile nature of the research instrument itself."

(Denscombe, M., 2007, p. 27)

To gather the most reliable information available, the author gathered information from sources such as Privacy International, the Electronic Frontier Foundation and Google itself. All other research data collected should be confirmed by authorities or approved institutes before writing the Project. To ensure of the reliability of all information, the author compared the results found by using triangulation and compared them with results already mentioned in other sources.

3.2 Research Families

Research families are qualitative and quantitative data as well as deskwork and fieldwork which can be drawn from the primary or secondary data.

3.2.1 Qualitative and Quantitative Data

"Qualitative research is concerned with collecting and analysing information an as many forms, chiefly non-numeric, as possible."

(Blaxter, L., 2006, p. 97)

Qualitative data are those which focus on the quality of a source and the data provided instead of providing a lot of information. These data were needed for an objective outcome of the Project because this Project involved numerousness opinions and criticism from many different sources such as the Electronic Frontier Foundation and the German Government. As qualitative data, the author quoted the laws, such as the European Data Protection Act of 12 July, 2002 and the United States Safe Harbor Act of July, 2000. Moreover, the researcher used the Google Privacy Policy website to gain information about their End User License Agreements in order to provide a good quality outcome.

"Quantitative research is concerned with the collection and analysis of data in numeric form. It tends to emphasize relatively large-scale and representative sets of data."

(Blaxter, L., 2006, p. 102)

By quantitative data is meant the amount of information. These information can come from all sources and include statistics and opinions, but the emphasis is on quantity not on quality. The advantages of quantitative data are that the findings are easily analysed and evaluated by computers which allow conclusions that can be considered as a solid and objective research because of a large amount of available data. The disadvantage is that a large number of quantitative data is needed in order to be representative for an evaluation which could not be accomplished because of the limitation of time.

3.2.2 Primary Data (Field Research)

"Refers to data collected from original sources and not already published sources."

(Remenyi, D., 1998, p. 98)

The primary data refers to new information which does not exist already. The data is unique and can be collected using methods such as questionnaires, interviews, observations, experiments, etc.

The author limited his field research to short questionnaires for getting an impression of people using Google and how they feel about privacy and safety in the world wide web and why Google is, despite criticism, so popular. Morever, because the author's Project is a critical analysis of Google's behaviour, he made an experiment to demonstrate whether it is easy to find sensitive information about individuals or not. Furthermore, he discussed the outcomes of the experiment with the participants in a focus group in order to get an impression of Google's user behaviour and awareness and to evaluate why Google is, despite criticism, so popular.

Detailed description about the questionnaire, experiment and focus group can be found in chapter 3.3 *Research Methods*.

3.2.3 Secondary Data (Desk Research)

"Refers to data obtained from already published sources such as directories or databases."

(Remenyi, D., 1998, p. 132)

Secondary data are data which already exist in different sources like academic journals, textbooks, case studies, as well as online content. They will be collected and evaluated for a new research.

In regard to the Project, the author put emphasis on secondary data, especially in terms of the legislation. He limited the geographical area for the laws to the European Union and the United States of America because of the limitation of time.

"Documents can be treated as a source of data in their own right - in effect an alternative to questionnaires, interviews or observation."

(Denscombe, M. 2007, p. 134)

The author used documents for the examination to the Project question because these are an important source of secondary data. Furthermore, there existed already a lot of content, especially in terms of the criticism about Google, in academic journals, such as "The Economist" as well as on the internet from websites, such as the eff.org. These documents supported the author with profund knowledge and background information of secondary data. Moreover, the author made use of books about Google, such as "The Google Economy" by Ralf Kaumanns (2007) and internet-related textbooks which contain information and statistics about internet user behaviour such as "The Future of the Internet: And How to Stop It" by Jonathan Zittrain (2008).

The author also used the google.com website for secondary research on Google's history, future plans, their product line and statistics as well as for their general terms and conditions and Googles' EULA (End user license agreement).

3.3 Research Methods

There are five different types of research methods: (Denscombe, M., 2007)

- **Questionnaires**
- Interviews
- Observation
- Documents/ secondary data
- **Experiments**
- **Focus groups**

3.3.1 Questionnaires

"Questionnaires rely on written information supplied directly by people in response to questions asked by the researcher."

(Denscombe, M., 2007, p. 158)

A questionnaire was an important research method for the authors' Project. With the questionnaire, the researcher wanted to get wider opinions about the user's concerns when using the internet and especially when using Google. The response rate was quite high, about 115 of 150 completed questionnaires returned to the researcher. The questions included were only general in order get an overview why people are using the search engine, although the company is hardly criticised in terms of data protection. The author sent the questionnaire mainly to students and colleagues of work, because they tend to use the computer more often and this helped the researcher to get wider and profund opinions about their concerns when using the internet and Google. The outcomes played an important role to get an overview of the customer behaviour and awareness of Google and an answer to the question why the company is, despite criticism, so popular.

3.3.2 Experiment

"An experiment is an empirical investigation under controlled conditions designed to examine the properties of, and relationship between, specific factors."

(Denscombe, M., 2007, p. 166)

As mentioned in the Justication, the author made use of a field experiment. A field experiment will *"be carried out in a natural environment rater than in a laboratory."*

(Denscombe, M., 2007, p. 167)

He set three age groups (18-24), (38-44), (60+). Because of a limitation of time and because the author wanted to gain a basic overview on how much sensitive information can be found and how these information can be found, the author limited each group to two persons. Those persons were asked by the author to type their own name followed by the town each person is living in into the Google Search Engine. The participants were then allowed to Google their name, as well as using all other Google products, such as Street View and Maps for 20 minutes which gave them some time to google some information about themselves. Afterwards, the participants were asked to write down the outcomes (i.e. ticking boxes of what they have found) anonymously by mentioning their age group only on a piece of paper.

These outcomes also played an important role to the Project objectives, as one of the authors' main outcome is to analyse Google critically in terms of online safety, privacy and personal data on the internet as well as to see the reaction of the people using Google. (besides legislation)

With the outcomes of this experiment he aimed to analyse which types of websites are included in Google and are transparent for any individual to search for information about other persons by using Google as well as how much can be found.

3.3.3 Focus Groups

"Focus groups make particular use of group dynamics. They consist of small groups of people who are brought together by a 'moderator' to explore attitudes and perceptions, feelings and ideas about a specific topic."

(Denscombe, M., 2007, p. 175)

After the experiment, he discussed the outcomes with the participants in a focus group to get information about their opinions and perceptions on data protection legislation, feelings about their information published on the internet and an answer to the question why people use the Google Search Engine, although it is hardly criticised.

3.4 Ethical Issues

"There is a general expectation that researchers should operate in an honest and open manner with respect to their investigation. Codes of conduct include reference to providing fair and unbiased analysis of findings and, crucially in the current context, researchers are expected to avoid deception or misrepresentation in their dealings with informants or research subjects. They are expected to be open and explicit about what they intend to collect data for the purposes of an investigation into a particular topic. Furthermore, they are expected to tell the truth about the nature of their investigation and the role of the participants in that research."

(Denscombe, M., 2007, p. 205)

The author had to consider also ethical issues in his Project which are as follows:

- Respect the rights, dignity and privacy of those who are included in the research
- Operate with honesty and integrity
- Legality and fidelity

Primary research which includes confidential data from Google and other organisations has to be dealt with confidence. The author had to operate with honesty and had to mention someone else's work if he will include it in his research Project, as well as respecting the rights and privacy of people who are included in the Project. He had to stay objective during the whole Project, otherwise the outcomes would have personal influences and an own opinion.

In regard to the experiment, the author had to guarantee the anonymity and he had to respect the rights and privacy of the participants. He had to make sure that all of them will be inducted and that they knew that the outcomes of them are included in the Project. The author gave each person a synonym, such as a1, b1, c1, etc. The outcomes must not contain personal data and pictures, they were summarized and stated under each age group in the Project.

It was very important for the author to gather a lot of good-quality and valuable information which allowed him an objective outcome to the Project question and further recommendations for customers of Google to protect their data.

Chapter 4
Analysis of primary and secondary research findings

4.1 Identification of reasons why Google is, despite criticism, so popular

4.1.1 Google's story of success

"We are generally not talking about our strategy because that's strategic."

(Google.com/corporate, 2009)

According to comScore (comscore.com/press, 2007), more than 700 million people around the world are using the internet regularly. Furthermore, the internet is gaining an immense growth because of an increase of the number of online user due to the growing possibilities of the internet. According to Kaumanns R. (2007), Google has nowadays more than 8 billion websites indexed and processes more than 200 million search enquiries everyday.

Google Inc. has been founded in September, 1998 by Sergey Brin and Larry Page who where IT students at Stanford University, USA. Their family, friends and especially Andreas von Bechtolsheim, a co-founder of Sun Microsystems invested in the development of Google. In 1999, after long-term and complicated negotiations, two of the most important risk investors, Perkins and Sequoia Capital invested $ 25 million in Google. Since September 1999, Google works together with AOL and Netscape. In June 2000, more than a billion websites were indexed in the search engine, Google was then the leading search engine on the market. Google, did not invest the money in advertising but in the development of the search technology and the Googleware as well as in the expansion of the company. (Google.com/corporate/history, 2009)

According to David Drummond, the senior vice president of Google (2007), the company has made it from a 2-men garage company to one of the leading companies worldwide because of a strong brand image and an excellent user experience. Its original activity, the search engine moved to a secondary position. According to him, Google is nowadays a strong brand on the internet and positions itself more and more to a meta information company which earns money by acting as an intermediary via advertisements. The company collects more and more data to make it worldwide accessible for everyone, especially in terms of education, public health and politics. Most people use Google or Google Apps for their everyday life. He says that due to Google, the advertising and marketing sector on the internet changed a lot because of the automatisation of online advertising (Drummond, D., 2007, FocusMoney, 2008). Kaumanns states that Google takes over more and more companies in the future and will be among a few others the leader on the internet.

4.1.2 Reasons for Google's success

According to Kaumanns, R. (2007), the reason why Google is so popular, is because of the user experience. The search engine is available in 120 languages and its design is known for its simple user interface. Furthermore, it is because the company abandoned advertisement from their apps as well as from the initial page of the search engine. Through the search engine one can find useful tools, such as Google Maps, Street View, Calendar, Docs, Mail, translation service, etc. All these tools provide an excellent user experience.

Drummond said that 4 factors were the key to Google's success:

1. *Technology. Along with its innovative approach to page ranking, Google is a purpose-built hardware company, building all its own servers from components it buys directly for their manufacturers.*

2. *Business Model Innovation. By perfecting the nature of targeted ads, Google not only has created a highly effective revenue generator, it has produced what it hopes to be a better experience for its users. It is Google's goal to make their targeted ads at least as relevant and useful to*

users as the search results themselves.

3.   *Brand. According to Drummond, a European study recently determined Google to be the number one most recognized worldwide brand. Indeed, Google has become a verb ("I can't wait to get home and Google him") which poses real challenges to a company seeking to protect the strength of its mark.*

4.   *Focus On The User Experience. Product decisions at Google are driven by optimizing for the user experience first and for revenue second. The folks at Google firmly believe that the better the user experience, the more easily money will follow.*

(Drummond, D., 2007, FocusMoney, 2008)

4.1.3 General outcomes of the questionnaire

The researcher sent his questionnaire to students and colleagues of work because they usually use the computer more often and this helped the researcher to get wider opinions about their concerns when using the internet and especially when using Google. This questionnaire only included general questions about the Google Search Engine because the author wanted to give an answer to the question why millions of people use Google, although the company is hardly criticised in terms of data protection.

According to the questionnaire outcomes, 71% use the internet for more than five years and only 2% for less than six months. The average of hours that the people questioned connect to the internet is between 27 - 33 hours which also includes connecting to the internet at work. However, most of the questioned people stated that they use the internet for entertainment, followed by communicating with others. Educational and/or work related purposes are ranked third, followed by making purchases.

The fourth question was to rate the level of concern over internet related issues. Most people said their major concern is that their profile, photos and phone numbers are easily accessible for others while the stealing of personal data was not a concern at all. Strangely enough, most people said that finding information about a person is not a concern at all. All other concerns were ranked as an average concern, except for the accessibility of pornography which was ranked as a lower concern.

Most people also said that they use either the Google Search Engine (63%) or MSN Live Search (19%) and 43% of all people questioned stated that they have googled themselves and/or other persons. 37% of them found nothing at all, the remaining 63% found mostly phone numbers, addresses and photos.

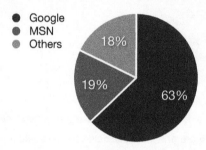

● Google
● MSN
● Others

18%

19%

63%

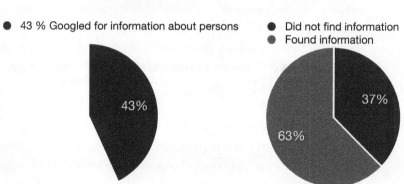

● 43 % Googled for information about persons

● Did not find information
● Found information

43%

37%

63%

78% of all people questioned who use the Google Search Engine, said that they feel safe when they use the Search Engine, 6% did not know and the remaining 16% said that they do not feel safe because they have heard of data misuse in the news and/or are a victim of data misuse or think that Google collects to much personal data.

In conclusion, these outcomes show that most of the questioned people use the internet for more than five years and spend approximately 30 hours per week on the internet for entertainment and social purposes. Furthermore, they show that a major concern for most people is that one can find easily user sensitive information but most of them do not see the stealing of information as a concern. 63% of the questioned people who googled themselves found sensitive information about themselves. Only 16% said that they do not feel safe using Google because they have read articles in the news and/or have made own experiences. This showed the researcher that the people questioned see their data published on the internet as a concern but clearly most people are not aware of data misuse and the criticism existing about Google. Google is, despite criticism, so popular because of an excellent user experience, because it is the most common search engine or because most people just do not know that the company is being criticised in terms of data protection.

(See also page 42, chapter 4.4, break one for additional opinions on reasons why Google is, despite criticism, so popular)

4.2 The relationship between how Google works with user sensitive data and in what way the company depends on these data

Google is being criticised of institutions such as the EFF and Privacy International of depending and distributing too much data but the company refuses the allegation of violating the rights of individuals. (eff.org, 2008)

4.2.1 The dependence of data and use of data

Because Google does not possess its own media, but is rather acting as an intermediary between user and companies/information, Kaumanns, R. (2007) says that Google depends on a huge amount of data from user as well as from companies which will then be used from both sides for advertising in order to earn money.

Through strategic and tactical partnerships with other companies, such as AOL, Netscape, YouTube, Vodafone, Ask Jeeves, Samsung, Sky, eBay, Hewlett-Packard and others, Google reaches data of millions of user. (google.com/corporate, 2009)

Jonathan Zittrain (2008) says that the company would not exist today if they have not collected these data, because a lot of companies are advertising within the Google search engine via Google AdSense and AdWords. These companies do so, because they know that Google has the most data of user as well as the most partnerships with other companies which give them a wider market to advert for their products. Furthermore, Google's business model is *to turn a seeker into a purchaser*, which cannot work without seeking people because otherwise there won't be any company advertising in Google's search engine and Google would make losses. So in order to earn money, Zittrain says, Google is dependent and uses user data to display matching adverts in the search engine results of the enquiries of user. For each click on an advert, Google gets a certain amount of money from the company adverting.

4.2.2 The data Google collects

The EFF (eff.org, 2008) and Privacy International (privacyinternational.com, 2008) say that there are lots of informations Google collects. The researcher found on the Google website (google.com/privacy, 2009) information about what data and information are saved and sent to Google when using the search engine or any application. According to Google's Privacy Policy, in just one search enquiry, Google collects the country code domain, query, IP address, language, safe search, server log, date, time, clicks, URL, and when searching by using additional preferences it can include street address, city, state and the postal code. For a Google account one has to provide an alternative e-mail, personal picture, etc. Google checkout goes even further: full legal name, credit card number, debit card number, card expiration date, card verification number, billing address, phone number, bank account number and social security number are required. Google Calender sends all events with informations like: who is going, who is invited, comments, descriptions, date and time to Google. Google Desktop can be also also as an instant messenger, but all chats will be sent to Google. The application Goog411 which is a VOIP application such as Skype which sends all phone numbers to Google. Google Groups sends all information about the groups joined to Google. Picasa, which is an application of Google where user can upload the recent holiday photos on the internet, saves all photos online and sends them to Google. Google Mobile sends the location information (GPS) directly to Google. Google Health sends all medical records, such as the doctors, conditions, prescriptions, race, blood type, weight, height, allergies, test results and more to Google.

Furthermore, the Privacy Policy states how long the information will be saved. Cookies (information saved on a webserver) sent to Google which were saved in 2008 for example, will expire in 2038. (Google.com/privacy, 2009)

According to a report of the EFF (eff.org/deeplinks, 2008), this clearly infringes the Data Protection Acts and when a company cooperates with a government it would also infringe the Human Rights Act, as it - according to the report - happened in China, where the government cooperated with Skype, a VOIP application. According to the EFF, all phone calls done and suspicious messages written via Skype were saved and automatically forwarded to the Chinese Government.

According to a report of The Economist (2007), Viacom, a media company that owns MTV, Comedy Central and the Paramount film studio has demanded in a deal for $ 1 billion the personal data of millions of Google's YouTube user, so that it could conduct a detailed examination of the viewing habits of YouTube user around the world. Google refused the deal because of a threat to expose deeply private information which violates the American Video Privacy Protection Act.

4.2.3 The legal side

As mentioned earlier, the data collected by Google will be used, according to Google, for advertising purposes only, but why does the company need data like phone numbers, calender entries and personal chats? Critics, such as the EFF, Privacy International and the Electronic Privacy Information Center agree that this is a violation of the data protection act (eff.org et al., 2008). Google has for each application seperate EULA's, which allow them to ask for any information they want if the user agree on these EULA's. According to the European Data Protection Act of 12 June, 2002 (Article 29, section 1), sending information and saving data on an external webserver is only permitted if the user consents and has access to these data. Google is legally allowed to save information if the u-ser agrees and if these information are not made publicy available.
Distributing and selling sensitive data no matter for what purpose, however, is a violation of this Act. According to the European Data Protection Act, only the Go-vernment can ask for specific user data from a certain user from a company if this helps the Government to clarify a murder or terroristic activities.

4.3 Investigation of Google in terms of data privacy

"European regulators found that companies such as Google and Yahoo violate several Data Protection Acts" (Ryan Singel, Member of the EFF, eff.org, 2008)

Therefore, the Data Protection Working Party of the European Union published an opinion on data protection issues related to search engines. (00737/EN WP 148)

"For the independent data protection authorities in the EU, the increasing im-portance of search engines from the perspective of data protection is reflected in the increasing number of complaints received from individuals (data subjects) a-bout potential breaches of their right to a private life. A marked rise in requests has also been noted from both data controllers and the press about the implicati-

ons of web search services for the protection of personal data." (European Data Protection Working Party, 2008)

In this dissertation one can find a lot of different types of criticism on Google. This chapter evaluates the criticism with the help of an experiment and compares it with the legal side, i.e. in what way Google is or is not infringing the European Data Protection Act of 12 July, 2002 and the United States Safe Harbor Act of July, 2000, as well as other laws that apply.

4.3.1 Criticism on Google

The EFF, Privacy International, the Electronic Privacy Information Center and others are accusing Google of infringing the Data Protection Acts by including user-sensitive information in their search engine results as well as sending and saving information and data that is being processed when using a Google application. Furthermore, the EFF says that because Google is the most used online search engine worldwide, the company acts monopolistic and perpetrates these laws. (eff.org, et al., 2008)

4.3.2 Outcomes of the experiment

The researcher had six participants of three age groups who were asked to google their own name followed by the town the person is living in and write down all the information found. The participants were allowed to use the Google Search Engine and webpages linked in the search results as well as all Google-Apps but not the search within social networking sites such as Facebook or StudiVZ. The emphasis for the researcher was not only on how much one can find but also on how it can be found.

The findings are as follows:

Age group 18 - 24 years:

The two participants of this age group found the most information of the three age groups. Full user profiles with personal information and a lot of contact addresses such as instant messenger numbers, phone numbers and e-mail as well as their home addresses were accessible without actually logging in to a social networking site. According to the participants of this age group, they have found the most information on yasni.de and 123friends.com.

Age group 38 - 44 years:

This age group found less information than the younger age group. One of the participants of this age group obtained most information from yasni.de while the other participant found the information on various websites. Both participants also found their personal phone number and e-mail address of their office at work.

Age group 60 years and above:

The participants aged 60 and above said that they really struggled finding something. One participant found personal data on stayfriends.de which is a website where one can find former class mates and the other participant only obtained his phone number and address from an online telephone book.

The findings of the participants were linked in the Google Search Engine results to other webpages, only in two cases personal photos were on the first page of the Google Photo Search. However, those photos also came from other websites and not from Google itself. In both cases of the age groups 18 - 24 and in one case of the age group 38 - 44 photos and personal information were according to the participants obviously obtained from social networking websites such as Facebook, StudiVZ, MySpace and others. Furthermore, the participants said that two certain websites were linked in the search results in all cases. These websites were yasni.de and 123friends.com, which according to the participants summarized all personal information from social networking sites, instant messengers, online phone books, etc and presented the outcomes on a single page, although social networking sites are password protected. The age group 18 - 24 years stated afterwards that they found lots of information on websites were they cannot remember registering at.

This experiment showed the author that there is a lot of sensitive data and information accessible for everyone on the internet but however, these data were not made accessible by Google, but rather by other websites linked in the search results.

4.3.3 Analysis of the criticism about Google in relation to the legislation

Author's note: The United States of America have no comprehensive data protection legislation. Instead, a mix of legislation, regulation and self-regulation is utilised which are similar to the European Data Protection Act of 12 July, 2002. The US Department of Commerce also developed the "Safe Harbor Act" in July, 2000 in consultation with the European Commission. Organisations can sign up to the scheme which will then be certified as offering adequate protection under the terms of this Act. However, the signing up to the Safe Harbor Act is not obligatory.

According to Google's Privacy Policy, the company signed up to the US Safe Harbor Act at 15 October, 2005 and is registered with the US Department of Commerce's Safe Harbor Programm. (export.gov/safeharbor, 2009)

Article 1 of the European Data Protection Act of 12 July, 2002 states that *"the purpose of this Act is to protect the individual against his right to privacy being impaired through the handling of personal data."* This Act applies to the collection, processing and use of personal data by ... Article 1, section 3 *"private bodies in so far as they process or use data by means of data processing systems or collect data for such systems, process or use data in or from non-automated filing systems or collect data for such systems, except where the collection, processing or use of such data is effected solely for personal or family activities."*

<u>Google includes user-sensitive information in their search engine.</u>

The researcher could not find any detailed information in the European Data Pro-tection Act and the United States Safe Harbor Act as well as in any other legisla-tion of the United States of America that prohibit the inclusion of user-sensitive information in a search engine. According to Drummond (2007), all information come from other websites, such as Facebook and MySpace, which will be in-tegrated in the results of the search engine, which means that it is everyone's own responsibility to control what data one has published online. By agreeing to the terms and conditions of these websites, one agrees that these information will be used and/or published, etc for other purposes. This depends on the terms and conditions one agrees to.

<u>Google sends user sensitive information and saves these on an external webser-ver.</u>

Article 29, section 1 of the European Data Protection Act says that *"the collection, storage or modification of personal data in the course of business for the purpose of transfer, in particular when this serves the purposes of advertising, the activi-ties of credit inquiry agencies, trading in addresses or market or opinion re-search, shall be admissible if (1) there is no reason to assume that the data sub-ject has a legitimate interest in excluding such collection, storage or modification, or (2) the data are retrievable from generally accessible sources within the geo-graphical area of the data subject or the controller would be permitted to publish them, unless the data subject clearly has an overriding legitimate interest in ex-cluding such collection, storage or modification."*

This means that the individuals have a right to access the information held about them and they must not be kept any longer than necessary. Furthermore, they must not be transmitted outside the European/US Economic Area and have to be saved adequate. Also, the person whose data is stored has to consent to the processing of those data by agreeing to the terms and conditions of their search engine and applications.

According to Google (google.com/privacy, 2009) the user has access to his or her own data (such as the data on an e-mail account), but not to the webserver of Google where the data is stored, however they can be requested for a fee of US$ 10. The data are stored on webserver by Google are according to Google within those geographical areas, however the researcher could not find the exact locations for the United States of America and the European Union - according to lots of less-quality websites this information is a secret kept by Google and only a few people know where they are located exactly.

Google saves all personal information and data (search enquiries, addresses, etc) with the user's IP address.

Article 3, section 1 of the European Data Protection Act says that *"Personal data" means any information concerning the personal or material circumstances of an identified or identifiable individual."*

However, the IP address itself is under the European and the United States Safe Harbor Act, not personal data. But according to the European Data Protection Act on protection issues related to search engines of 4 April, 2008 an IP address can become personal data when combined with other information such as address, name, etc. Because one has to register for most Google's apps, the IP address becomes personal. However, the storage of IP addresses combined with personal information does not infringe any of those Data Protection Acts, on the internet it is rather a standard to save these addresses and information for security reasons as well as for demographic purposes such as counting visitors, their countries of origin, etc. According to article 29, section 3 of the European Data Protection Act on protection issues related to search engines, it becomes a violation of the data protection act when these information will be made accessible in combination with the IP address for other persons as well as the distribution of those information to other companies.

Google Street View is infringing the personal rights of individuals.

In the United States Constitution of 15 December, 1791, there is a legal principle stating under the fourth amendment that there is no reasonable expectation of privacy in public places which is in relation to the Fourth Amendment of the United States' Constitution which *"protects people, rather than places and therefore its reach cannot turn to presence or absence of an intrusion into any given enclosure."* Therefore Google Street View is legal in the United States, although there exists also a lot of criticism against this application.

Article 6b, section 1 of the European Data Protection Act says that *"monitoring publicly accessible areas is allowable only in so far as it is necessary (1) to fulfil public tasks, (2) to exercise the right to determine who shall be allowed or denied access or (3) to pursue rightful interests for precisely defined purposes and if there are no indications that the data subjects' legitimate interests prevail."*

In the European Union Google started capturing cities until many governments, such as the German Government and independent institutions, such as the EFF raised criticism, because in the EU, taking pictures of individuals in public places is not permissible under EU Privacy Laws, unless the individuals are notified. Furthermore, Street View is infringing article 8 of the European Convention on

Human Rights of 3 September, 1953 by taking pictures of individuals in public places.

Article 8 of the European Convention on Human Rights (ECHR):

- Right to respect for private and family life -

1. *"Everyone has the right to respect for his private and family life, his home and his correspondence."*
2. *"There shall be no interference by a public authority with the exercise of this right except such as in accordance with the law and is necessary in a democratic society in the interests of national security, public safety or the economic well-being of the country, for the prevention of disorder or crime, for the protection of health and morals, or for the protection of the rights and freedoms of others."*

Google stopped Street View in Europe for now. (google.com/privacy, 2009)

<u>Google integrated a censorship in the Chinese search engine.</u>

Google intregrated a censorship in lots of countries (google.com/support, 2009). In the US, Google censors all search results that comply with DMCA-related illegal complaints (Digital Millenium Copyright Act). In Germany and France, Nazi, anti-semitic and radical Islamic websites have been censored by Google.

In China, Google adheres to the Internet Censorship Policies of China. The internet censorship is because of the government's effort to neutralize critical online opinions.

However, under the article 10 of the European Convention on Human Rights and under the article 19 of the Universal Declaration of Human Rights of 10 December, 1948, this inhibits the freedom of speech.

According to Google.com, the company does so to prevent people to use the search engine for topics and websites that infringe other laws, for example those that regulate the freedom of opinion of Neo-Nazis in Germany.

<u>Google's EULA's are infringing the data protection act.</u>

(giving Google the right to distribute, publicly display and use any content submitted or posted by their user for advertising purposes)

Article 4, section 1 of the European Data Protection Act states that *"the collection, processing and use of personal data shall be admissible only if permitted or prescribed by this Act of any other legal provision or if the data subject (the individual) has consented."*

Article 4a, section 1 states that *"consent shall be effective only when based on the data subject's free decision. He shall be informed of the purpose of collection, processing or use and, in so far as the circumstances of the individual case dictate or at his request, of the consequences of withholding consent. Consent shall be given in writing unless special circumstances warrant any other form. If consent is to be given together with other written declarations, it shall be made distinguishable in its appearance."*

The researcher found lots of different contract laws for the individual States of the United States of America. However, in all States the data subject has to consent the processing and use of personal data. (hg.org/commerc, 2009)

As mentioned earlier, the EFF and Privacy International are accusing Google of their EULA's because paragraph 11 (giving the company the right to distribute, publicly display and use any content submitted or posted by their user for advertising purposes) infringes, according to them, the Data Protection Acts. (eff.org/deeplinks/archive, 2009) Google changed those EULA's for most of their applications, such as Google Docs, but for some they still apply, such as Google Chrome (google.com/privacy, 2009). However, Google uses the data only when the user permits this by agreeing to the terms and conditions. Using non personal information is legal for advertising purposes according to US and EU Data Protection Acts. As long as the information distributed and publicly displayed are not personal, it is legal.

Article 7 of the European Data Protection Act states that *"where a controller causes harm to the data subject through the collection, processing or use of his personal data that is inadmissible or incorrect under the provisions of this Act or other data protection provisions, such controller or its supporting organisation shall be obliged to compensate the data subject for the harm thus caused. This obligation to provide compensation shall not apply if the controller has exercised due care in accordance with the circumstances of the case concerned."*

4.4 Analysis of Google's customer awareness and behaviour

The outcomes of the questionnaire showed the author that many of the people questioned see their data published on the internet as a concern, but most of them do not think that someone would steal it. The outcomes of the experiment showed the researcher that especially the younger generation (25 years and younger) found a lot of sensitive data about themselves, such as photos, addresses and user profiles.

With the participants of the experiment, the author discussed in advance how they feel about the stealing of data and data protection in particular and to find out why people are using the Google Search Engine, although the company is according to lots of experts and critics hardly criticised for their lack of data protection for individuals. After the experiment, the researcher and the participants discussed about the experiment's outcomes.

According to the participants, the answer to the question of why they think Google is, despite criticism, so popular is quite simple, they see Google as the best and most accurate search engine and other search engines do not offer applications such as Maps, Calendar, Street View or a free translation service.

Furthermore, they feel that Google is the most customer friendly company, because their search engine is not overcrowded with advertisements and all of their applications are free to use. According to them, the criticism of Google is not a major concern at all to them because they feel that in today's society lots of companies are under criticism and that one cannot trust everthing published in articles, especially those published on the internet, because everyone can online let one's mind wander and publish his thoughts in blogs. However, they feel that data protection has become one of the most important issues over the recent years in industrialised countries because of a possibility of a misuse of personal data (see chapter 4.2.2 *The data Google collects* for an example). The participants also stated that in this case (i.e. the experiment's outcomes), that data protection legislation goes beyond governmental control and that therefore everyone is responsible on his own for his own data in terms of publishing them on social networking websites or online calendars, etc.

In relation to the outcomes of the experiment, the younger participants did not react with suprise to the findings. They rather knew that will find a lot of sensitive information but they said that they did not know that these information are accessible within the Google Search Engine. The participants aged 60 and above however, were suprised, although they did not find as much as the other participants. They seemed to be annoyed and said that they cannot imagine why their data is accessible for everyone.

This discussion showed the researcher that especially the younger generation is aware of their sensitive data published on the internet which is a concern for them but they see this as rather usual in the 21st century and that it is also everyone's own responsibility to control the flow of their data. In terms of behaviour, the participants stated that there are no rules or guidelines, rather morals and an ethical behaviour so that it causes no harm to other persons. Furthermore the participants pointed out that people are using Google because they see Google Apps as the best and most accurate applications which are all free to use. *(see also chapter 4.1.2 Reasons for Google's success)*

4.5 Recommendations for Google's customers to protect their data

This chapter provides recommendations from experts for internet user to improve the protection of their data. This chapter is linked to the outcomes of the questionnaire in chapter 4.1.3 and to the experiment in chapter 4.3.2 and in regard to the outcomes of the evaluation of the data Google collects in chapter 4.2.2.

The EFF (eff.org/wp, 2006) and Safetynet (safetynet.app.org, 2009) suggest that when using the internet one should never give away his or hers name, especially in connection with other personal data such as address, credit card number, etc. However under special circumstances, i.e. when shopping online, one should pay attention to the encryption of the website. If the website is not encrypted, other users and computers can access the website and steal the credit card number with security number, especially when accessing the internet through an unencrypted wireless network. User should always create a password for their wireless network. Also, one should deactivate cookies, because these submit the IP address, country, query, server log, language and content of the page one is connected to and save it on an external webserver to load the website faster and react to individual user settings.

Furthermore, user should read the terms and conditions before registering and not just tick the button, because in the case of Google, the user retains copyright but give Google a perpetual, irrevocable and worldwide licence to reproduce, adapt, publish, publicly display and distribute any content that he or she submits, posts or display on or through the services. This paragraph in Google's EULA's is hardly criticised and has been changed for most Google apps except for the Google browser Chrome.

According to the EFF and Safetynet and in regard to the experiment, websites such as Facebook, MySpace, StudiVZ and Blogger should be deactivated for anyone that is not a friend or relative, because these pages are included in Google search engine results. The quantity of information on a profile depends on the user and should be limited and not too personal, but the researcher's questionnaire and experiment demonstrated that most user tend to put at least an instant messenger address, a photo album and the personal address on these pages.

Furthermore, users should be aware of the pages they are registered at. When the website or service is no longer used, one should deactivate the account, otherwise it will be kept online and information are still be available for others. Pages such as yasni.de and 123friends.com collect all information from ICQ, MSN, Facebook, StudiVZ, MySpace, Skype, Google and others and make it accessible for everyone when searching for a certain person, which was demonstrated in the author's experiment.

According to the EFF, the problem is that when a person has good internet skills and wants to find something about another person, he or she will presumably find something. According to CareerBuilder.com, there is a trend that when applying for a job, potential employer google information about potential employees. 33 % of the recruiters who use social networks in their hiring process (Facebook, StudiVZ, Myspace) have rejected candidantes based on what they found. (CareerBuilder.com/article, 2008)

To see what information one can find about oneself, the best way is according to Kaumanns (Kaumanns, R., 2007) to Google his or hers own name. However, according to Safetynet (safety.app.org, 2009) the automatic sending of sensitive user information to Google or any other website goes beyond user control in most cases.

Chapter 5

Conclusion

5.1 Review of research objectives

5.1.1 Objective one

Identification of reasons why Google is, despite criticism, so popular.

The researcher evaluated the main statements of different articles about Google and came to a conclusion that Google is so popular because of the user experience and four key factors of success such as technology, business model innovation, brand name and the focus on the user experience. Furthermore, the participants of the author's experiment feel that Google is, despite criticism, the most customer friendly company because of free-to-use applications, the elimination of advertisements in their search engine and because it has the most accurate search results.

The questionnaire showed that the people questioned either do not know about the criticism surrounding Google privacy law issues or - according to the discussion with the participants of the author's experiment - do not see the criticism as a concern at all, but rather as something that happens to a lot of companies quite often nowadays and that one cannot trust everything published.

5.1.2 Objective two

Evaluation on the relationship between how Google works with user-sensitive data and in what way the company depends on these data for their business.

The researcher came to a conclusion that because Google does not possess its own media and is therefore acting as an intermediary between user and companies/ information. As mentioned in chapter 4.2.1, Google's business model is *to turn a seeker into a purchaser,* therefore, Google depends on a huge amount of customers, so that companies are likely to advertise within search results in the Google Search Engine and a huge amount of data and information from customers to display matching adverts in the search engine results of the user's enquiries in order to earn money. The secondary research findings in chapter 4.2.2 (*The data Google collects*) demonstrate the huge quantity of information and the different types of data that will be collected by Google.

The terms and conditions of Google's products are stated in the End User License Agreement of each product which state also information about what kind of data will be collected by Google when using this product. However, researching the Data Protection Act of the European Union as well as the United States Contract Law showed that Google is legally allowed to save information if the user consents and if these information are not made publicly available.

5.1.3 Objective three

Critical analysis of Google's behaviour in relation to the European Data Protection Act and the United States Safe Harbor Act. (among other laws)

The primary research (i.e. the questionnaire and the experiment) findings demonstrate that 63% of the people questioned who use Google as their search engine googled themselves and/or others found sensitive information about themselves and/or others. The experiments' outcomes emphasize on the questionnaires' outcomes and show that it is rather easy to find and collect information by using the Google Search Engine and/or other GoogleApps. Especially the youngest age group of the experiment found a whole range of sensitive information while the oldest age group struggeled in finding something. In all cases, two certain pages were linked within the search results of the participants which, according to them, summarize all personal information about a specific user.

The secondary research, the analysis of Google's behaviour, are in this case the outcomes of the questionnaire and the experiment in relation to the European

Data Protection Act of 12 June, 2002 and the United States Safe Harbor Act of July, 2000.

Google adheres to the laws in most of those cases. However, due to the fact that the United States of America have no comprehensive data protection legislation and mix of legislation, regulation and self-regulation, as well as the Safe Harbor Act instead, there was not always an exact law that applies or not applies to the assertions about Google's behaviour. In the case of Google Street View and in the case of the censorship policy of Google, not the Data Protection Acts, but rather the Human Rights Act and the Universal Declaration of Human Rights apply.

In the case of the censorship that Google integrated in the Chinese search engine, Google is presumably infringing article 19 of the Universal Declaration of Human Rights, because the censorship inhibits the freedom of speech. However, Google does so to adhere to the Internet Censorship Policies of China and in other countries to prevent people to use the search engine for topics and websites that infringe other laws.

5.1.4 Objective four

Analysis of Google's customer awareness and behaviour.

The discussion about Google's customer behaviour emphasize on the primary research findings of the questionnaire and of the experiment. The participants stated Google is being used because they see Google as the best and most accurate search engine and the participants as well as 84% of the people questioned feel safe using Google. Only 16% of the people questioned stated that they do not feel safe using Google because of criticism and/or own experiences. However, the participants of the experiment came to a conclusion that data protection legislation goes beyond governmental control and that everyone is responsible on his own for his data published on the internet.

The participants of the youngest age group of the experiment found the most sensitive data but did not react with suprise when they found all the information, they rather knew that they will find a lot sensitive information, although they admitted that they did not know that these information would be included in search engine results. The participants aged 60 and above were suprised and seemed annoyed of the fact that information about them is published on the internet, although they have not found as much as the other two age groups.

This analysis about Google's customer behaviour showed the researcher that most of the questioned people as well as the participants of the researcher's experiment use Google applications, especially the search engine, regularly and that people are either not aware of the criticism surrounding Google privacy law issues or that the criticism does not have an impact on the loyalty of their customers.

5.1.5 Objective five

Recommendations for Google's customers to protect their data.

The secondary findings of this objective are in relation to the outcomes of the experiment and the questionnaire. The research of the objectives one to four showed that Google is collecting a large quantity of data but nevertheless, they are adhering to the legislation. This objective was rather meant to be descritive, not analysed because the researcher's aim was to give recommendations for customers of Google and the internet in general to protect their data, therefore this objective has not an exact outcome. Previous research showed that internet user / customers of Google have quite a lot of sensitive information published online and in order to protect one's own data, the researcher found a lot of helpful hints from internet privacy experts for example the deactivation of cookies and the encryption of websites. However, they said that it has also to be mentioned that the automatic sending of user information goes in most cases beyond user control. Moreover, the researcher found out that there is a trend of recruiters using social networks in their hiring process.

5.2 Concluding remarks

The aim of the researchers' project was to assess to what extent Google users are aware of the criticism surrounding Google privacy law issues and to what extent those are valid. On the one hand, Google adheres to the privacy law acts, but on the other hand, some cases go beyond data protection legislation. Therefore, the author also researched the European Human Rights Act of 1998, the Universal Declaration of Human Rights of 10 December, 1948, the European Data Protection Act on protection issues related to search engines of 4 April, 2008, the European Convention on Human Rights of 4 November, 1950, the Constitution of the United States of America of 17 September, 1787 and several contract laws of the United States of America. The outcomes of investigating these additional laws are that Google infringed article 8 of the European Convention on Human Rights by taking pictures of individuals in public places. However, Google stopped capturing for Street View in Europe. Moreover, Googles' censorship in the Chinese search engine infringes article 19 of the Universal Declaration of Human Rights and article 10 of the European Convention on Human Rights, because the censorship inhibits the freedom of speech. However, because Google does so to prevent people to use the search engine for topics and websites that infringe other laws (e.g. Neo-Nazis, terrorism, underage porn), the company is allowed to integrate a censorship within a search engine. Therefore, the criticism surrounding Google privacy law issues are not valid.

Primary research showed that most Google users are either not aware of the criticism surrounding Google privacy law issues or that the criticism does not have an impact on the loyalty of their customers at all.

The experiment clearly demonstrated that no specific internet skills a needed in order to find information about another person. Furthermore it demonstrated how much information can be found and where these information can be obtained from. In all cases the participants of the experiment obtained the data from third-party websites linked in the search results in the Google Search Engine. These information come from other websites due to the fact that Google does not possess its own media but is rather acting as an intermediary between user and companies. The data Google collects will be sent to and saved on an external webserver which is according to the European Data Protection Act of 12 July, 2002 and the United States Safe Harbor Act of June, 2000, legal as long as the user has access to the data, which they have.

Because the information come from third-party websites, Google cannot be accused of infringing the Data Protection Acts. On one hand the user hisself is responsible for his information published on the internet, such as the information on social networking sites. On the other hand, the experiment showed that although the social networking sites are password protected, websites such as yasni.de and 123friends.com hack those pages and summarise all information and make user information available for everyone.

After finishing the research, especially the several data protection acts in relation to Google's behaviour, the author of this Project was really suprised. He had not expected the outcome to be like this because the EFF, Privacy International and the Electronic Privacy Information Center, which are all mayor organisations in the internet and privacy sector, are more or less wrong by saying that Google infringes Data Protection Acts. Opinions and perceptions on this topic may vary and some people think that Google's behaviour is unacceptable, but the author's objective was to analyse Google's behaviour in relation to the legislation on data protection.

While most companies have an ethical conduct, Google's corporate motto and ethical conduct is as mentioned earlier *"Don't be evil"*. Google has been voted by Ethisphere in 2008 (ethisphere.com/ wme2008, 2008) to the most ethical internet company. However, by providing a basis for censorship, monitoring and tracing of information of user as well as possessing thousands of server filled with sensitive data of millions of user from all over the world, no matter if Google adheres to the Data Protection Acts or not, the researcher has been left with the question if this behaviour can be considered as ethical.

12,438 words

Bibliography

Textbooks

SAUNDERS, M., 2000. *Research Methods for Business Students.* 2nd edition. Harlow: Financial Times / Prentice Hall.

BLAXTER, L., 2006. *How to research.* 3rd ed. Berkshire: Open University Press.

REMENYI, D., 1998. *Doing Research in Business and Management - An Introduction in Process and Method.* Wilshire: The Cromwell Press Limited.

DENSCOMBE, L., 2007. *The Good Research Guide.* 3rd ed. Berkshire: Open University Press.

KAUMANNS, R., 2007. *The Google-Economy.* Norderstedt: Books on Demand GmbH.

ZITTRAIN, J., 2008. *The Future of the Internet - And how to stop it.* London: Yale University Press.

EVERETT-CHURCH, R., 2002. *Internet-Sicherheit für Dummies.* Oldenburg: MITP Verlag.

BLAKLEY, B., 1999. *An Introduction to safe Computing with Objects.* London: Addison-Wesley Longman.

Journal articles

REYNOLDS, M., 2008. Google's new web browser Chrome. *In: The Economist San Francisco,* (10).

SMITH, C., 2008. Google's Virtual world. *In: The Economist San Francisco*, (8).

DRUMMOND, D., 2008. Google schießt Giftpfeile. *In: Focus Money*, (2).

KOPYTOFF, V., 2008. German Towns saying "Nein" to Google Street View. *In: San Francisco Chronicle*, (10).

Government publications (also from web pages)

BUNDESDATENSCHUTZBEAUFTRAGTER (DE), 2008. *Google Street View: Bundesdatenschutzbeauftragter gegen Ausleuchtung persönlicher Lebensumstände - für strikte Verwertungsgrenzen bei Geodaten.* [online] http://www.bfdi.bund.de/nn_531002/DE/Oeffentlichkeitsarbeit/Pressemitteilungen /2008/PM_21_08_GoogleStreetView.html Accessed on: 11/01/09

DATA PROTECTION WORKING PARTY (EU), 2008. *Opinion 1/2008 on data protection issues related to search engines. (00737/EN WP 148).* Brussels: EC.

DATA PROTECTION WORKING PARTY (EU), 2002. *European Data Protection Act of 12 July, 2002.* (95/46 EG), (97/7/EG), (98/27/EG) (99/34/EG). Brussels: EC.

EUROPEAN CONVENTION ON HUMAN RIGHTS (ECHR) (EU), 1953. *Protection of Human Rights and Fundamental Freedoms: European Convention on Human Rights Act of 3 September, 1953.* Rome: EC.

UNITED NATIONS (ALL MEMBER COUNTRIES), 1948. *The Universal Declaration of Human Rights of 10 December, 1948 (UDHR) (217 A III).* New York: UN.

UNITED STATES CONSTITUTIONAL CONVENTION (US), 1791. *The Constitution of the United States of America: The Bill of Rights of 15 December, 1791.* Philadelphia, PA: USCC.

UNITED STATES DEPARTMENT OF COMMERCE (US), 2000. *United States Safe Harbor Act of July, 2000 in relation to EU Directive 95/46 EC.* Washington, DC: USDC.

Web pages

ELECTRONIC PRIVACY INFORMATION CENTER (EPIC), 2009. *Press Releases: Google.*
[online]
http://epic.org/
Accessed on: 14/02/09

ETHISPHERE, 2008. *2008 World's Most Ethical Companies* [online]
http://ethisphere.com/wme2008/.
Accessed on: 23/02/09

COMSCORE, 2007. *comScore releases Search Engine Rankings.* [online]
http://www.comscore.com/press/release.asp?press=1745
Accessed on: 15/12/08

PRIVACY INTERNATIONAL, 2007. *A Race to the Bottom: Privacy Ranking of Internet Service Companies.* [online]
http://www.privacyinternational.org/article.shtml?cmd%5B347%5D=x-347-553961
Accessed on: 17/01/09

PRIVACY INTERNATIONAL, 2009. *Top News: Google.* [online]
http://www.privacyinternational.org/
Accessed on: 19/01/09

ELECTRONIC FRONTIER FOUNDATION (EFF), 2006. Six Tips to Protect Your Search Privacy. [online]
http://www.eff.org/wp/six-tips-protect-your-search-privacy.
Accessed on 27/02/09

CAREERBUILDER.COM, 2008. *One-in-Five Employers Use Social Networking Sites to Research Job Candidates.* [online]
http://www.careerbuilder.com/share/aboutus/pressreleasesdetail.aspx?id=pr459&
sd=9%2F10%2F2008&ed=12%2F31%2F2008&cbRecursionCnt=1&cbsid=e0967
ffc33684b908b5870932a12ea56-287515215-RN-4.
Accessed on: 23.02.09

GOOGLE PRIVACY CENTER, 2009. *Privacy Policy.* [online]
http://www.google.com/privacypolicy.html
Accessed on: 07/01/09

GOOGLE CORPORATE INFORMATION, 2009. *Company Overview.* [online]
http://www.google.com/corporate/
Accessed on: 08/01/09

GOOGLE CORPORATE INFORMATION, 2009. *Google Milestones.* [online]
http://www.google.com/corporate/history.html
Accessed on: 08/01/09

HG WORLDWIDE LEGAL DIRECTORIES, 2009. *Commerical Law - Guide to Commercial Law.* [online]
http://www.hg.org/commerc.html
Accessed on: 03/03/09

ANDERSON, N., 2008. *Google on Chrome EULA controversy.* [online]
Arstechnica.com
http://arstechnica.com/tech-policy/news/2008/09/google-on-chrome-eula-controv
ersy-our-bad-well-change-it.ars
Accessed on: 19/12/08

SAFETYNET, 2008. *AAP Resources.* [online]
http://safetynet.aap.org/

Accessed on: 28/02/09

ELECTRONIC FRONTIER FOUNDATION (EFF), 2008 - 2009. *Deeplinks: Google.* [online]
http://www.eff.org/deeplinks/archive
Accessed on: 17/12/08

EXPERIMENT: What data can you find by using Google?

a1 + b2 = aged 18 - 24
a2 + b2 = aged 38 - 44
a3 + b3 = aged 60 and above

Please google yourself (name followed by town you live in) for 20 minutes and tick what you have found.

	a1	b1	a2	b2	a3	b3
Address	x	x	x	x	x	x
House (Maps/Street View)	x	x	x	x	x	x
Hobbies	x					
Photos	x	x	x	x		
Recent schools	x	x		x		
Interests	x					
Birth date	x	x	x			x
E-mail address	x	x	x	x		
List of friends	x			x		
ICQ number	x	x		x		
Skype-ID	x			x		
MSN ID	x	x				
Phone number	x	x	x	x	x	x
Mobile number		x				
Wishlist (Amazon.com)	x					x
eBay user profile	x	x	x			
Events (Calender)			x	x		
Address (of work)		x	x	x		x
E-mail address (of work)		x	x			
Other (please write down in the box)						

Which three websites / apps linked by Google provided the most information?

	a1	b1	a2	b2	a3	b3
1.	yasni.de	Face-book	Face-book	Stayfriends.de	Online phone book	Online phone book
2.	123fri-ends	StudiVZ	Google Calender	yasni.de	-	other
3.	StudiVZ	yasni.de	company website		-	-

QUESTIONNAIRE: Do you think you are safe on the internet in terms of your own privacy? (Approx. 10 minutes) - please return to: sven.elmers@gmx.de

1. For how long have you used the internet? (please circle)

less than 6 months	6 months to one year	1 - 2 years	2 - 5 years	5 + years

2. How many hours per week, on average, do you connect to the internet?

3. For which of the following purposes do you use the internet? (Please circle)

Entertainment	Educational
At work	Personal finance
Current events (news, etc)	Travel-related
Product information gathering	Making purchases
Communicating with others	

Other: (please state) _____

4. Rate your level of concern over the following internet issues:
   5 = major concern, 1 = not at all a concern)

My profile, photos, phone numbers are easily accessible	
It's too hard to find something (In terms of information about a person)	
Someone could be monitoring what I do online	
Pornography is too easily accessible	
My personal information will be stolen	
Someone will misuse the personal information I give them	
I am concerned about online banking	
I don't know how my information (when registering) will be used	

5. Which search engine do you use? (please circle)

MSN	Google	Yahoo
Lycos	AskJeeves	Other

6. Have you ever googled yourself (or any other person)? (please circle)

yes	no

7. If yes, please circle what you have found.

Address	Images of your house
Hobbies	Photos
Recent schools	Interests
Birth date	E-mail address
List of friends	ICQ number
Skype-ID	MSN ID
Phone number	Mobile number
eBay user profile	Nothing at all

Other: (please state) _____

8. Do you feel safe when using Google? (please circle)

yes	no	don't know

9. If not, please state shortly why you don't feel safe when using Google.

_____
_____
_____
_____